# BOK'S GIANT LEAP

## ONE MOON ROCK'S JOURNEY THROUGH TIME AND SPACE

Written by

## NEIL ARMSTRONG

Illustrated by

## GRAHAME BAKER SMITH

Crown Books for Young Readers
New York

When I was a boy, I dreamed I was
**high above the Earth** with
only clouds for company.

For as long as I could hold my breath,
I floated.

But I could not hold
my breath forever.

I'd wake and watch
the Moon drifting
by my window,
wondering at all it
must have seen and
imagining how it
was made.

I learned that when the Earth was very young—
4.5 billion years ago—it was involved in a great
celestial fender bender.

A smaller planet smashed into Earth!

The collision sent billions of tons of
molten rock into orbit. Over hundreds
of years, this rock merged and stuck
together to form a sphere.

The Romans called it Luna.
The Greeks, Selena.

We call it MOON.

It was a turbulent and terrifying time for the Moon.

Lava flooded up from below its surface, filling giant craters like hot soup in a bowl. Geysers of erupting gas shot globules of molten rock into the sky.

Half a billion years of chaos passed before the Moon
began to quiet down. As the crust cooled, it cracked.

A piece of fresh young basalt broke off
from a larger rock and rolled away.

I call him

BOK.

Geologists—people who study rocks—
have a saying: "Rocks remember."

History is recorded in the minerals and
marks of each boulder and pebble. During
the next four billion years, Bok would see
and remember many things.

He saw the Sun rise in the east and parade
majestically across the sky to set in
the west.

Occasionally, new stars would burn with
a fiery brilliance against the velvet
blackness of space.

Constellations changed their
shape as stars were born,
burned for millions of
years, and disappeared.

600 million years
went by, and then an
asteroid struck Bok!

It catapulted him into
the sky toward a crater at
a terrific height and speed.

Bok held his breath for
as long as he could.

But eventually he fell.

Skipping a time or two, he came to rest on the rim of a small crater. Part of his right side broke off when he landed. All his basalt neighbors were left far behind. He didn't know if they had been vaporized, melted, or blasted far away.

Bok was alone.

It took him about half a billion years to get over the experience and settle down before, once more, turning his gaze to the sky.

The Earth was still there. It was in a state of terrible upheaval. Volcanoes turned its atmosphere to smoke, but when this cleared, Bok could see the blue of newly formed oceans.

Continents would creep out of the
sea, **linger** a while, and then slip
once more below the waves.

And swimming deep beneath those waves was the teeming, earliest complex life on Earth.

Another billennium went by.
The Moon was quiet now.
Nothing ever happened.

But on Earth, plants appeared
on land. Amphibians developed,
ventured out of the sea, and in time,
learned to live above water.

Dinosaurs roamed the Earth. But they
disappeared almost before Bok noticed them.

An entire chapter of Earth's history.

There and gone in the blink of
**170 million years!**

Bok was then a little over 3.5 billion years old and starting to feel sleepy.

Through tired eyes, he glimpsed the rise of the mammals. He saw the Earth turn into a giant snowball beneath the grip of the Ice Ages.

Just before sleep enveloped him, he saw
a new creature standing on two legs,
holding a flint-tipped spear . . .

. . . staring in wonder
at the Moon.

He slept deeply as the Moon continued to accompany the Earth on its endless journey around the Sun.

And so he missed the unfolding story of humankind.

He missed Plato and Hypatia.

Charles Darwin.

Maria Mitchell.

Konstantin Tsiolkovsky
and Bessie Coleman.

He missed the **birth** of the boy
who grew up to climb aboard a
rocket destined for **the Moon.**

Bok couldn't have guessed that his nap
would end with a **rude awakening**
early one lunar morning.

A peculiar creature was lifting him
with an unusual metal device.

He was roughly thrown into a box
with some acquaintances he knew
only slightly.

Then the lid was closed
and it was dark.

Bok felt a brief force.

Then a sense of **weightlessness** for a time.

Flames outside the window blotted
out the blue of the Earth as the
space capsule streaked through
the atmosphere, blazing
like a comet.

The heat stirred a
deep and ancient
memory in Bok.

A memory from
so long ago it
seemed like
a dream.

He remembered
the early days of
the Moon. The chaos
and fire of its birth.

He remembered . . . he had been
a part of the Earth!

Millions of people all around
the world were watching.

Holding their breath until they
saw the space capsule floating beneath
three bright parachutes splashing into
the arms of the ocean . . .

. . . returning all on board
safely to the place from
which their journey began.

And now you know some of Bok's history.
You can go and see him at a museum in the
United States—or at least a part of him.
A chip off the old Bok, you could say!

Perhaps you might try and imagine what he is
thinking as he looks out at us looking at him.

Does he see us as something new and different
on this Earth that he's watched for so long?

Or, like the dinosaurs, just another species that
exists for a brief moment of geological time?

After all he's seen, Bok must be very wise.
But if you ask him about the Egyptian pharaohs,
don't hold your breath waiting for an answer.

## He missed them!

# The Moon

The Moon has fascinated us for as long as we've been in existence. It is Earth's only natural satellite—the only object that orbits our planet that isn't man-made. Although it spins around just like the Earth does, we always see the same face of the Moon because it rotates in exactly the same time as it takes to orbit the Earth.

Many scientists believe that the Moon was created around 4.5 billion years ago when a planet roughly the size of Mars collided with the Earth. The impact sprayed rocky debris into space, which eventually gathered together to form our Moon. At first it was very volcanic there, with lava erupting all the time. But over millions of years, things settled down and became quiet. The only disturbance was whenever an asteroid or comet struck the Moon, creating impact craters that we can still see on its surface.

# The Earth

Our planet is about 100 million years older than the Moon, and formed when smaller rocks collided and clumped together. The impacts created a lot of heat, and for a while Earth was a boiling ocean of lava. But eventually things started to cool off, and a crust formed on the Earth's surface. Water vapor escaped, and soon clouds gathered. As rain started to fall and meteorites containing water impacted Earth, the crust was flooded, creating oceans.

The first life on Earth were very simple organisms that developed about 4 billion years ago. They evolved into much more complex life-forms in our oceans and, eventually, on land. Dinosaurs appeared about 247 million years ago and dominated the planet until some kind of catastrophe. Most scientists think a massive asteroid crashed into what is now Mexico.

Mammals started to evolve in new ways when the dinosaurs died out. *Homo sapiens*, or modern humans, first walked the savannahs of Africa around 300,000 years ago.

Since then we have spread across the world and learned a great deal, thanks to ingenious minds like philosopher Plato, mathematician Hypatia, naturalist Charles Darwin, astronomer Maria Mitchell, pilot Bessie Coleman, rocket scientist Konstantin Tsiolkovsky—and even the first man to walk on the Moon: Neil Armstrong.

# One small step . . .

Neil Armstrong's journey to the Moon started long before he climbed aboard his spacecraft. Born in Ohio in 1930, he first fell in love with flying when his dad took him to see an air show—and by the time he was 16, he'd gotten his pilot's license.

After attending university and flying in the Korean War, Neil became a test pilot, flying all sorts of cutting-edge planes as they were being developed. But Neil wanted an even more exciting challenge than that, and in 1962 he applied to NASA to become an astronaut in the space program.

In 1966, he piloted the Gemini 8 spacecraft, achieving the first-ever successful docking of two vehicles in space. But minutes later, the two spacecraft began to spin wildly—and Neil saved the lives of himself and his crew when, while under enormous G-forces, he wrested back control.

Safely back on Earth, Neil was put in charge of the Apollo 11 mission, joined by two other astronauts, Buzz Aldrin and Michael Collins. The United States and the Soviet Union were in a race to try to land on the Moon first.

On July 16, 1969, Apollo 11 launched from Kennedy Space Center in Florida. Four days later, having orbited the Moon 13 times, Apollo 11's lunar module set down on the Sea of Tranquility—which is actually an impact crater filled with basalt rock, not an ocean.

On July 20, Neil became the first person to walk on the Moon, with 600 million people watching on TVs around the world. His first words were:

Together, he and Buzz spent 21 hours on the Moon, collecting rocks to take back to Earth for study—including Bok.

On July 24, 1969, the crew returned as heroes, splashing down in the Pacific Ocean in Apollo 11's command module.

"That's one small step for [a] man . . .

. . . one GIANT leap for mankind."

In 2006, NASA announced Neil as an Ambassador of Exploration and presented him with a small fragment of rock he had brought back from the Moon. During Neil's acceptance speech, he gave the rock a name—Bok—and imagined all the amazing things it must have seen throughout the solar system's history. Neil's wife, Carol Armstrong, had the idea of turning it into a book, and this is the result. Bok is now on display at the Cincinnati Museum Center's Museum of Natural History and Science.

Text Adaptation and Illustrations © 2021 Grahame Baker Smith
and Neil A. Armstrong Trust, Carol Held Armstrong, Trustee
Design copyright © Hodder & Stoughton Limited, 2021.
Original Text © 2006 Neil A. Armstrong Trust, Carol Held Armstrong, Trustee
Original Text by Neil A. Armstrong, 18 April 2006

The publisher would like to thank the following for permission to reproduce their pictures:
pp. 36–39 NASA; p. 38 (left) Purdue University Archives & Special Collections.

Visit us on the Web! rhcbooks.com

Educators and librarians, for a variety of teaching tools, visit us at
RHTeachersLibrarians.com

*Library of Congress Cataloging-in-Publication Data*
Names: Armstrong, Neil, 1930–2012, author. | Baker Smith, Grahame, illustrator.
Title: Bok's giant leap : one moon rock's journey through time and space /
Neil Armstrong ; illustrated by Grahame Baker Smith.
Description: New York : Crown Books for Young Readers, 2021. |
Audience: Ages 4–8 | Audience: Grades PreK–3 |
Summary: "Based on a speech Neil Armstrong gave upon receiving the Moon rock he named Bok,
this unique picture book tells the story of how the Earth and the Moon came to be.
Includes facts about the Earth and the Moon." —Provided by publisher.
Identifiers: LCCN 2021005435 (print) | LCCN 2021005436 (ebook) |
ISBN 978-0-593-37886-1 (hardcover) | ISBN 978-0-593-37887-8 (library binding) |
ISBN 978-0-593-37888-5 (ebook)
Subjects: CYAC: Moon rocks—Fiction. | Earth (Planet)—History—Fiction.
Classification: LCC PZ7.1.A75 Bo 2021  (print) | LCC PZ7.1.A75  (ebook)
DDC [E]—dc23

MANUFACTURED IN CHINA
10 9 8 7 6 5 4 3 2 1
First American Edition

Early sketches
of Bok